PLEASURE

KELVIN C. BIAS

ARCHIVE
ZERO

ARCHIVE ZERO | NEW YORK | 2025
www.archivezero.com

Published by Archive Zero, LLC

Paperback ISBN: 978-1-955722-28-5
Hardback ISBN: 978-1-955722-29-2
E-book ISBN: 978-1-955722-27-8

Cover design by Robson Garcia Jr.
Formatting by Polgarus Studio

for the release

CONTENTS

"If every person in every country had a friend in every other country, the prospects for war and a host of other world problems would approach zero. Let's approach zero together."

Kelvin C. Bias

PLEASURE

I AM THE SKY

The orange horizon,
A comfort, a fragile friend.
She pierces my defenses.
She upholds the dimensions.
I am infinite blue, the
Breath remnant of God.

Pleasure lies in the small things.
The bebop blown from a saxophone,
The touch of her fingers when alone.
We are all children of the sky,
We ply wares born of rain and lightning,
Primordial delinquents with DNA.

Aloft in time, Earth sings, believes.
Her minions gather on her surface.
They dance, mate, succumb to fate.
Here I lie, here I die, and here I *live*.
I am the sky. Beyond the clouds.
So, inhale, breathe love.

RUNAWAY

The beach has one tree
But two footsteps. Dented,
Then smoothed. Carved,
Then disappeared by swells.
We, two humans, run free,
Laugh in our altogether,
Suctions for the tropical sun.
Our passion, our runaway
Attraction to the good life
Spreads simple, coconut dreams.

The lagoon holds our extremes,
No room here for secrets.
The outer waves lash with intent.
The inner ring binds our paradise,
While clouds bow to our sky.
Kiss, embrace, clasp, insert,
These keys wetter than silk
In an eternal thunderstorm.
We fish, we eat, we tend our fire.
We are the only inhabitants.

WHISPERS

Resolute thoughts
Plunge into
Dark waters
At midnight.
No one hears.
No one knows
The hidden truths.
In this darkness
Rests the realm
Of whispers.
Unrequited lovers,
Unaccomplished
Goals, untaken trips:
These fish
Swim in the depths.
We yearn, we strive.
Everyone breaks
The surface
When primed.

DRIFT

I am wood on your sea.
The crest of one wave
Ascends then descends
Into the next. I bob and
Weave year after year,
Guided by undulations.
Temptation leads to
A passing bottle,
A fellow denizen
Of ocean royalty.
If the ship sinks,
I will remain a
Plank of flotsam
In your jetsam lee.

MIDNIGHT

The point-of-view is raw,
Back and shoulders bared
For the world to stare.
It's midnight somewhere.

The watchers and their views,
The preachers and their pews.
The analog data, the analog curves.
There are stars, planets, and moons.

Like ripples on a pristine lake,
The far side of Earth and its rakes
Mend to their own devices,
Gardens of delight take flight.

Lovers won't be the last ones in the room.
Lovers watch their channel for the rest of June.
Smiles, delectations, adulation.
The clock strikes, and we wind temptation.

MOONLIGHT BORDER

Darkness kowtows
To the light. The
Void has no luster
Without precious
Beams, bailiffs of the
Exquisite border.
So goes the moon,
Its light defined
By the blackness.
We plunge into
The unknown only
Because we have
Nocturnal companions.
Hail, moonlight.

DANCES

What dances
Can I spool
To make you
Frantic?
Rhythmic,
Asymptomatic,
Aromatic,
Autoerotic,
Robotic?
Like geography,
The feet pilot
The performance.
The mind slides,
Thrill mode
Activated, a
Natural reaction
To you, the
Powerful aphrodisiac.
Mind upon
The needle,
We spin happiness
On the floor, in
Rhythmic galore:
The beat implores.

DREAMS

You sit upon the throne,
The goddess of dreams.
Multitudes wish they
Held your magnetic sway.
Each night we meet,
Each night, we're sweet.
No one dare compares.
The intensity of our
Trysts is never forlorn.
We are the amusement
Park *and* the ride.
We are greater than
The lion and the pride.
When slivers of light
Pierce the gallant room,
I resist the call to reality.
I want to exist in fantasy.
Dream, birds, dream.

AWAKEN

The green hedge,
Perfectly trimmed,
Perfectly macabre,
Spews blood from
A central hole
Like a dragon
Armed by a
Volcano's kiss.
In the maze of
Destiny, I want
To hold your hips,
To pump life into
Imagination, to
Entice trances.
Awaken my dear.

SHADOWS

Of shadows and stone,
The old bone longs
To be chewed again,
To be the object of
Rabid attention.
The lascivious hounds
Of longing languish
In the fleeting night.
The dark moments
Must be tempered by
Waves of afterglow.
We are beasts of the
Silent forests at the
Edge of civilization's
Enchanting game.
We embrace the gloom.

SOFT

I'm never
Too tired
To make love.
Soft, your
Bare body
Elicits euphoria.
We wallow in
Its suave grace.
Fireworks fragment,
Cathode rays denote
Background noise.
We bend to satisfaction.

FAIR

Conceived
Somewhere
At the L.A. County fair,
I revel in existence.
Pride is my dagger,
Both my defiant strength,
And equal downfall.
Pomona has beautiful air.
I am heir to youthful fancy,
A bridge to a lucky eternity.
I am a destined May flower.
I am my own Ferris wheel.

GLIDE

My armor is yours.
Take it to the
Parapets of
Carnal imagination.
Smelt it to desire.
Hold passion fast
To your breasts.
Bring my bare body
To your keep, the
Lighthouse in the midst
Of frantic waves.
Leaven the proceedings
With libidinous elixir,
With calibrated positions
Fixed in the heavens.
The stars and their
Legions mass. And I?
I tremble, a calmed
Knight, then we
Glide into tomorrow.

LINGERS

She stood beneath sin.
A carefree spirit in heat.
I want her to stay.

IGNITES

Does she read
Alone at night
In her bedroom?
Or in broad
Daylight on
A bench in
Central Park?
The ribald reveries,
The whirligig notions,
The antidotes, and
Hopeful potions
Coalesce beyond rules.
I wander wherever
She wants. The flame is
Already ablaze, naked
Beneath the elements.
Morning song or evening dust,
The coming flood can't
Extinguish the sanguine rush.
She ignites this insatiable lover
From afar, close by, in between.
But I am one of many.
She is the free-spirited medium,
A conductor of lust.
She controls the demons.
She controls her legions.

They cannot control themselves.
She bemoans following reason.
She's their season.
They burn together every night.
They power the lights.
I am a single beam.

ECHOES

Hello…olleh!
Hello…oh…oh!
The mirror of
Sound washes
The canyon
Of previous
Ghosts. North Rim,
Bryce, Zion:
The red dirt,
The blue sky,
They listen.
The hogans
Uplift Earth,
The Great Mother.
The landscape dishes
Her own delight.

THE SMILE

Her smile drew me in,
Stretched me out,
Pushed and pulled,
Wrestled me to the floor,
Expunged my demons,
Ripped my clothes,
Sent pain to a distant
Galaxy, and rode the
Sunset for eternity.
I can't remember her name.

ATLANTIC BLUE

Her surface, placid,
She stares to the sky,
To me, to the distant
Sisters on other worlds.

The color as the strange bird
Lifts infuses the proceedings.
A happy state of pristine blue.
Preserve this moment, I the fish.

Ships are white dots awash with
A comet tail of foam; they scrub
The border between atmospheres.
Other birds of every hue fly somewhere too.

The heavens and the Atlantic merge,
Giving birth to the land, our human home.
Yet we still mingle in the air, the sea, the Earth.
We are the caretakers of rebirth.

ALTITUDE

High or low.
Mountains or
Below the sea.
We aim for
Our own
Altitude. Free.

FADE

The night sweats into day.
God's rays disappear darkness
On the horizon, a delirious line
Depicted by pink,
Orange, purple, gray.
The sins of the honky-tonk fade,
Liquor bottles ride tall within
The roadside Carolina pines.
Their detritus the only indication
Fun was had by all.

MOMENTS

The sound of springtime,
Fragments of eternity:
Figments of our mind.

CLOSED

No ropes. No safe words.
The door is closed, not open.
We are at one with each other,
Not bound by any others
Or tied like street flowers.
We aim for sacred pores,
Our mores ply consented poses.
Sounds filter into a disarmed room.
The lands of passion sing.
We are what we bring.

BENEATH

Beneath the sun.
Make love times one.
Beneath the moon.
Make love times two.
Beneath the greed.
Make love times three.
Beneath the stars.
Make love times four.
Beneath Kilimanjaro.
Make love times five.
Beneath Everest.
Make love times six
Beneath the sea.
Make love times seven.
Beneath the trees.
Make love times eight
Beneath the eaves.
Make love times nine.
Beneath the pyramids.
Make love times ten.
Equal to the universe.
Make love times eleven.
Because beneath the floor,
When the clock strikes
Twelve, we can't anymore.

TREES

We are insects
To the gigantic
Telephone poles
Of the Pacific Northwest,
Visible only when
We bleed our
Putrid waste
Into their streams.
The trees would
Rather we procreate
Beneath their canopy,
Spread seeds of
Another kind, people
Born to care for
The green kingdom,
Or at the very least,
Fertilize the soil,
Needed contraband for
All of our souls.

SILENCE PIERCED

The crinkling sounds of a cockroach
Or a trapped mouse waft inside as
The powder blue sky mates with the sun.
The low critters bask in air-conditioned stasis.
The lone man in Room 304 wishes
He was *nekkid* with a gorgeous woman,
Piercing the silence like the cotton ball clouds
On the far side of drawn curtains.
Let the world hear these longing thoughts.
A hospital attached to a hotel or *vice versa*.
Nurses and their medical minions mince words,
Then they don't, the truth hurts.
Outside, in the azure sea, birds call.
I'd rather shout and pretend.

HUSH

Promulgate May lust.
Blind in bed, we cannot hear.
Silence is our trust.

PETALS

I watched from above.
Your legs limned like
Georgia O'Keefe petals.
I wish I had a camera:
Light and shadow,
Color and our magma.
Softness girds for love's battle,
Kaleidoscopic revelry
Dominates my imagination.
I'll sprinkle pink and white leaves.

SURRENDER

The troops amble the
Antiseptic halls, armed
With balloons, cakes,
Flowers, new babies.
The brightness of May
Executes its plan:
No one surrenders today.
There will be laughs,
Chortles, guffaws, jokes.
Food will be eaten,
Doses will be taken,
Doctors will reside in the
Bedside manner reserved
For queens and kings.
The polished floors will not
Be slippery, there will be
No ornery patients
Wandering the halls naked.
The dark green treetops
Will remain outside
The sphere of death,
Visitors will come and go.
Here and now lies the
Lifeblood of content.
Tomorrow's another day.

SLIP

Her blue slip
Slipped to the floor,
A nuclear bomb
Detonated to
Destroy the shy
Atmosphere of
Two potential
Part-time paramours.
"Do you like
What you see?"
The man and woman
Replicated characters
From an old movie scene.
He could almost hear
The projector—light
From an open window
Dotted the scene.
There would be no
Post-coital regrets.
The sparse room,
Infused with joy,
Turned into a cathedral.
The delicate hands, the
Heaving muscles,
The deep eyes:
They sang in tune,
Slips of flesh
Forever and a June.

DREAMER

The stars, the stars,
I awoke in the midst of stellar birth.
I was the interloper,
The confused man.
Colorful sentient light
Loomed mere inches away.
However, when I reached,
My hands grasped the void.

I stood up, a solemn soldier.
There was no roof, no floor,
Only a translucent walkway
Disappeared into the fringe on
Every side, every geometric plane.
I set one naked foot forward and
The other one followed out of habit.
With each step, a new prick of light appeared.

After an indeterminate interval,
The starfield morphed into a
Blue prism, and the pathway
Melted into the chamber.
Inside, I continued my stride,
Each footfall leaving a blue outline.
My body stretched in every direction,
Whole, then thin, in myriad permutations.

The scenery changed. Atmospheres swirled.
Against valiant wind, I stood atop Kilimanjaro.
1973 and the summit still bled ice.
Logic did not hold sway. The stars, the prism?
They were gone, soon Kilimanjaro too.
But then, she appeared, a brown goddess.
Persian, Ethiopian, Indian, Moroccan, Kenyan?
She took my hand, led me to a mighty dune.

She pointed to an oasis beneath the ridge.
"You're the gatekeeper of this land."
Her sari wrapped tight against her skin,
She led me to the blue salve.
At the edge, she pushed me into forever.
Karmic ripples disturbed the pristine surface,
When I rose from the depths, all turned white.
She wasn't there, and I saw myself in a mirror.

The room went dark, time vanished.
The stars, the blue prism, Kilimanjaro, the oasis,
And in the top left, the girl. They returned
Like old friends with smiles and turbulence.
They shimmied in the mirror, laughed, cried, revered.
I, the man without a domain, where was this?
My community changed again. Angels held
Hands around the bed, and I resuscitated in heaven.

GOLDEN

I am a filament.
I am an element.

I am valuable
When you need it,
When you don't.

My valence never changes.
I am refined in your cauldron.
I render us sublime.
Can you not see the shine?

ACTIVE DOOR DO NOT BLOCK

I want to be awake when my mom sleeps
Because it's as if I have more time with her.
If she dreams, and I sleep, do we exist?
Different places, different spaces, different time.

Perceptions change in the gloam.
Deceptions fall away before an unblocked door.
I ask: Who's awake while I sleep?
Another person, another life, another wife?

There are times I want to be awake
While she sleeps because I don't want to hear
What she has to say, I block it away,
Be it the hard truth or an unjustified harangue.

We are minions of continuity, standing before doors.
Each one, a portal to some other kind of sleep,
Where dreams and reality coexist in an
Oppositional haze. Where pleasure rules.

ENDLESS

Of time and space,
I was once there, you, here.

We're endless.

By fate's luscious eye,
Our dimensions intersect.

We're endless.

Love communes in the passion room,
Without walls, barriers,
Watchers, or regulations.

We're endless.

We bloom within our curved
Spaces, hidden places,
Bow to sexual desire,
To serendipity's touch.

We're endless.

We perform kisses,
Acrobatics deep into
The nurturing night.

We're endless.

A view to an erotic thrill,
Naked together, we unwind
In this bewitching world line.

We're endless.

RAIN

Rain and pain are temporary.
The desire for touch lasts a lifetime.

Droplets form in the troposphere,
Divine entities destined for creation.

Tadpoles rise from the muck,
Creatures of wriggling joy.

Humanity gurgles from this mud,
Lightning and acids procreating.

So, when the firmament opens, contemplate.
The atoms of existence—*the why*—ablate.

WE LIE NAKED IN OUR OWN FLUID

I lie naked in my own fluid,
To remember a time we made time.
Now drawn curtains mock my stains
While shallow breaths elongate.
We don't have to be alone.
The ties and clothes can still bind.

We meet at midnight, cause a bind.
Different plans, the destination fluid.
I'd rather feel you than go it alone.
Shame flees as I scratch more time.
How many things can love elongate?
Over and over, we relish our stains.

Bottles and their elixirs stir miraculous stains.
High cheekbones keep me in a bind.
It's almost morning, our bodies elongate.
I want to curl into your ether, remain fluid.
Pressure and pleasure alchemize time.
We'll become diamonds, far from alone.

Reveal your aphrodisiac when we're alone.
Let's kiss for hours, make sustained stains,
Store them in a vault for the end of time.
I trust you here, I'd give you rope to bind.
When we're old they'll only draw fluid
So, now, over and over, please elongate.

Dance, rub, strip, flip, lick, elongate:
We do what we can when we're not alone.
Motions and minutes, the clocks are fluid.
We mark the hours by the number of stains.
Bind me in sacred lust; lust me in a sacred bind.
Let's repeat these moves from time to time.

The sun sets, the moon rises, it's our time.
Tonight, we won't sleep, the bed will elongate.
There will be no clocks, no hours to bind.
Despite the indiscretions of youth, we won't die alone.
Wrap our limbs, our magnificent stains,
I am yours, you mine, in unison our love's fluid.

Beyond time, we spread fidelity alone.
We elongate while our imagination stains.
Minds bind, we lie naked in our own fluid.

MORNING

Fall mornings are best.
Sun soft on the face, no tears.
We'll live in this grace.

DEW

When the proximity
Of your skin suffuses,
The sea levels rise.

The dew we create
Answers questions,
Proffers solutions,
Blows the walls
From the blue room.

Love rains upon us.
Love reigns beyond lust.

WINDS

The sounds of lovers,
The whispers of trees,
Turn up the volume.
They're speaking to me.

Where doth the winds come?

Alone after midnight,
I can't see their presence,
But they bite, they clean.

Where doth the winds come?

I feel nature's force.
Her strident canteen
Rips branches,
Swerves knees,
A river of enigmatic zephyrs.

Where doth the winds come?

I don't know the air's origin,
But make haste for home,
Pushed by an invisible stream,
To sleep with you...to dream.

Where doth the winds come?

HUM

We bask in the breathing room,
Without remorse, without fear,
Somewhere in a sleek hotel.
Our afterglow powers universes.
Your leg vibrates against mine,
Mine against yours. We hum,
Plum with every pleasurable sensation.
The *in flagrante delicto* aftermath doesn't
Need a reserve. We are the buzz,
The electric candy of eternal energy.
We levitate in smiles, fling tongues
Into satiated mouths as if yesterday
Never existed and tomorrow won't.
In this present, we are a presence,
A device of equal bearing with the world.
We hold hands—the only fabric
The sheets beneath our forms.
We are an aerial photograph in a museum,
Made in God's image, with God's POV.
Plug us in, tune us out, you can't win.

SKIES

Does your sky look prettier than mine?
Do we twirl under the same force?

I am restless beneath both gazes.
I am a boundless traveler with surprises.
I am seething with Love's divine supplies.

If our skies match, we're hers.

FLIGHT

One day, I'll dunk
A basketball
Like a Black
Messiah
Painted by
Ernie Barnes,
I'll have sex
With a girl in
Dad's pickup
Truck, I'll grow
Six inches my
Freshman year,
I'll graduate,
Go to college,
Get a degree,
Buy a new car,
Get married,
Buy a house,
Have kids, protest,
March, collaborate,
Instigate, castigate,
Recite poems by
James Weldon Johnson,
Play God's trombones,
Travel out of sight,
Witness a new creation,

Rocket to old age,
Sing dawn's early light,
Cure racism, disease.
Maybe one day...
I'll take flight.

GLOWS

Hot, like winter love,
My body glows in your sphere.
Beware the embers.

DRINKS BY THE BAR

The details, smeared by
Sadness, tarnished by memory,
Lurk in a bar lost to years and
One too many spills.
The floor with the decor
Straight from a *2001* odyssey
Remains a plinth like those stars.
My God, it's full of stars.
We were stars, young, fulgent with
Forever possibility. A fight
Broke out, I think, as I
Tried too hard with
Bad Norwegian.
A random rendezvous,
Flights to Europe,
A kiss, I ride gladness
Decades later, a smile,
Gratefulness, peace.
Though we didn't take,
The bar remains a memory.
My God, it's full of stars.
Ergo, I purse my lips and ask:
Where would I be, if not
For some drinks by the bar?

YOUR NAME IS...

Your name is...
Black-haired beauty.
Body hidden, but
I know it's there,
Perfect, spare.
I spied you from afar,
One night in the rain.
As I drowned pain,
Your allure led
Me beyond control.
Even now I remove
My clothes, utilize
My imagination,
Fall into the sheets.
Alas, it's all I have.
Nothing has been given,
Nothing taken away.
But I rise, hard in this
Knowledge: I will
Do it all over, I swear.

BRIGHT

Beauty oozes.
You stun the sun.

Bodies decay.
Yours is glorious.

Shine a bright light
On your mind.
Yours is the pinnacle.

I want to reach
The highest peak.
I'll be quiet, learn
Not to speak.
You're who I seek.

SEX ON A SATURDAY AFTERNOON

October sun floods the room with clarity.
Leaves flutter to the ground,
Nothing but candid reveries
In their desiccated veins.
Closer still, two lovers intertwine,
Intervene, interject new pleasures.
Their cogitations with motion
Shall fuel the world and this
Chapel is a dot on time's scale.
The stains are florid, the kisses lurid.
Blessed, the afternoon airwaves encode
Saturdays and Saturdays evermore.

NORWAY

Ibiza, London, Cannes, New York:
All roads lead to Norway,
To a mountaintop never scaled,
To beautiful times with a girl,
To different futures unfurled.

When we're 90, will we remember?
The fight at the bar, running out of gas,
The London rendezvous, the lights
At Pacha, summer thunderstorms,
The first night in our own Narnia?

I'll lock these in the memory bank,
The forgiving vault for posterity.
If the images and instances fade,
These words are merging testaments.
We looked glorious in the act.

DRENCHED

Spotted streets,
Slick with color.
Inside, we curtail
Our heat, the last
Clutch before offices,
Reality, strife, life.
The sky pours
Out her own feelings,
While we search
For our clothes.
Wouldn't it be nice
If we could wander
Outside as is,
Naked to the world,
Without recompense,
Without decomposed
Second guesses.
Without glued eyes.
Sometimes it pays
To get drenched.

ANCIENT

Tonight, we are ancient carnivores,
Ravished atoms of gnashing heat.
Tomorrow, we'll be found pressed
Together, fossils in flagrant pleasure.
Tonight, we'll fornicate before
The asteroid strikes, before Chicxulub's
Sister sears our ceremonial plants.
Tomorrow, we are a new species:
Bipedal creatures who destroyed it all.
Tonight, we'll spill life, skip, and fall.

ESCAPE REDUX

I abide on your island.
Your dark hair washes
Ashore with the kelp,
But you've drifted away.
The currents pooled, you whirled.
I could not hold the tides of
Time and convenience,
Still sightless from your beauty.

Let me escape with you.
Let me escape we two.

From dawn to dawn,
I long for your tokens.
Every sunset I see your ghost
Disappear into the waves,
Ride the swirls of whitecaps,
Then ascend to the silver stars.
Bring me to your shadow place,
Where an ocean of devotion hides.

Let me escape with you.
Let me escape we two.

DAWN

Why stay quiet?
No one's here.
The forest won't tell.
Let's scream,
Let's moan,
Let's dial
A few clouds,
Array an audience
Before the sun intrudes.
Darkness is a friend,
A fiend for satisfaction.
Let's bare beauty
Deep in the throes,
Until dawn graces
Our figures and we
Create an eclipse.

ELECTRIC WAVES

The euphoria device
Rests in that hidden drawer.
Leave it be. I am electric yen,
A machine of your choosing.

SAND

Grains of
Time and
Pressure
Grind my
Heart
Into tiny
Bits, only
To be
Reconstituted
When you
Walk across
That remote beach
On a distant
Blue planet
Where you wield
The lone Sun
To forge
A new me, an
Adonis, muscles,
Perfection,
Glistening
In awe of your
Nubile beauty,
Your talisman to
Fashion your way.
When you tire

Of me, be it,
Minutes, hours,
Days, weeks,
Years, millennia,
You must rub
My lantern until
I become
Particles
Captured
In your new
Hourglass.
Break the
Glass when
In direst need,
When time ends,
When we
Make love
Continuously
Into the final
Glorious days
And explode,
A birthed star,
Soon to become
Burning new sand.

BLUEBIRD

The buildings stare down at
The itinerant man in an
Itinerant city full of fleas.
The dogs of July consider tea.
Am I walking them or
Are they walking me?
I want to fly higher,
Rise into the cloudless sky,
See the world like a bluebird,
A prince of the sky, you and me,
Where we can all be free,
Where laws and love don't mix.
We are lady and lord,
Where all the problems are fixed.

CLOUDS

Cumulonimbus, cirrus,
These white seers,
Puffs of observant gas
Conquering the sky,
I wish there were nine
Aligned in a buoyant row
One upon another. For on
A distant day, we won't
Be able to wipe the rain
From our pores, to jump
Into bed delirious with
Carnal relish. So now,
We target titillating spots,
Exotic menu items
To make ourselves
Feverish. We work
Our horizontal horizon,
Call to the shroud, and
Disappear in a wisp,
Vapors ripe to reform.

HEAVY

The heart renders eternity.
It's the sky, sun, and moon,
The universe beyond.

Can you feel its weight in gold?
The compliant ease of its appliance?

Everyone lies heavy with a caring soul.
Let the heaviness operate your pump.
Let the heaviness burn the worlds.
Let the heaviness heal the wounds.

For the heart renders its weighty dream.

DREAMLESS

I woke up in the chair.
Restless, dreamless,
A blink, an instant.
My thoughts turned to
Other nights and
Other goddesses,
Their sacred love.
But only one remained.
I cried. Her memory died.
And then she wasn't there.

SHOCK

All systems do not go.
The light at the
End of the bed flickers.
The sights are not
For sore eyes.
Come see the wound.
The wound is deep.
I am become numb.

Shock allows for beauty.
For blessings in miniature:
Held hands, a gentle
Kiss on the forehead,
The rapture of care.
Bleed therapeutic love.
Cherish the unenviable tasks.
I am not become death.

GOBI

I have never seen
The pristine Gobi's
Whistling dunes,
Yet they call to me.
Beyond the curve
Of the Earth, outside
Time and mirth,
I hear their aeolian cry.
They, too, long for
Companionship, some
Energetic traveler to
Place footsteps on
Their backside, to
Massage their
Shifting spine,
Someone to
Delve into their
Hidden truths,
The buried
Remnants of
Civilizations past,
Someone to
Chat with about
The gleam on the
Ridge when the
Sun breaks the

Dark horizon.
I am this partner.
I commiserate
With the stark
Landscape, bathe
In desert glaze.
Two lonely souls,
The Gobi and I,
The Grand Wanderer,
We'll make a new song.

BLINK

Your summer visage,
Beauty that transcends space-time.
I don't want to blink.

BREATHES

Love heals.
Love deals.

Love breeds.
Love needs.

Love aches.
Love takes.

Love soothes.
Love moves.

Love climbs.
Love binds.

Love sheathes.
Love breathes...

JAMMY

Long ago London streets,
A girl, a view of the Thames,
Cobblestones and rendezvous.

Jammy chap, that's who.

The details are vague,
The kisses remain,
The pleasurable jams
And jellies, we rolled in bed.

Jammy chap, that's me.

Maybe she knew then,
That it wasn't to be.
Maybe I knew too,
Yet hung on her eyes,
Her smile, her
Scandinavian sensibilities.
I grin and realize:

Jammy chap, that's who I still am.

BELOVED

In spring, summer, fall,
I catch time and Hell for you.
Winter, too, beloved.

ECSTASY

I want more.
Continue.
Great.
I love being attacked.
Spray me with
Your ecstatic tears.
Ripple, bend, bounce.
We cannot stop.
Use me until
I become a desert.

DRILL

Your legs flush
Against the wall
Reveal splendor,
A house of wonder.
I, hammered by Eros,
Crave this night ritual.

We rewind, build on
Opportune orgasms, yell.
We are lecherous paste,
Attached to lithe thrill.
Charge the batteries.
I am your drill.

OPEN AIR

The May air portends
Long nights flush against my face.
Clouds make love overhead,
Produce their own families, while I
Saunter along the blue streets bound for
Blueberries and blue milk at the supermarket.
I tangle with the dark, push the unthinkable
Into its own black recess, and step again.
The sidewalk sheds its skin to meet mine.
I fail, but the midnight breeze brings peace.

SUNLIGHT

Seductive sunglasses slid
Down her face while
The denim short shorts
Inched up vagabond legs.
She glanced my way,
Elusive but tender.
An invitation?
A subtle dismissal?
She pulled out her
Lip gloss, the stick
Poked the exterior
Of her mouth like
Wildfire, kindle
For the sunlight,
A green indication.
Rays and selfies,
She disappeared
Into the social ether.
The East River glinted,
A reservoir to sin.
The plastic cup
Cupped her hand,
Ring on her right
Index finger, a demon.
Her white top need not
Fetch anyone more.

BOOGIE BOARDER

The sun owns the scene:
The foam, the swells,
The sensation of sand
Down my swimsuit.
Surfers eye the
Lime green dart
In the Pacific, the brown
Kid atop white crests.
Riptides be damned.
Blue skies, marine towers,
Catamarans shoot
Toward Newport
Circa 1986. The beach
And the *girls*, Huntington
Adrift—heaven—as the
Wave takes my suit.

THE MONTH OF MAY

Flowers brim beyond the rains.
The sun acts enraptured
By another girl. *He never learns.*
Insects return from a
Long winter's holiday.
Where did they go?
Somewhere in Mexico.
The cool breeze disappears,
Air conditioners return, and
Everyone knows we'll have to pay.
The heat's approaching, here to stay.
But like The Temptations say…

NIGHTCAP

Meet me at the bar,
On the counter,
At the hotel.
Don't falter, go
By nightshade,
By lust, by lamp.
The city beats,
And you, I need.
In the parallax of
The wee hours
Where anything goes,
Let's sidle up, get down,
Where nobody knows.
Let's unfurl your map,
Dance on moon-soaked streets,
Make our hearts skip.
I want to serve delight,
Engage a nightcap.

LIKE

I like to feel like a god.
I am of God, but *not* a god.
I am like cold strawberries on a summer day,
Like every wink and every smile, like Paris,
Like *Sesame Street* and Super Grover, like similes,
Like an indigo bunting blue against the sky,
Like butter and syrup on a stack of hotcakes,
Like Medjool dates in a sweet concoction,
Like a forest fire when nobody sees,
Like fisticuffs over a pretty girl, like rust,
Like snow on a winter's day, like butterscotch,
Like first class from Hong Kong to Tokyo,
Like vomit after the wildest night of your life,
Like masturbation in a tropical rainforest,
Like an unexpired passport, like money in the bank,
Like the guy in the rated R movie, like sin,
Like the man who knows exactly where to begin,
Like dark clouds over the Grand Canyon,
Like dismantled nuclear weapons, like peace,
Like white blood cells winning a war,
Like delusions when you're livin' the dream,
Like an alien invasion on a distant colony, like May,
Like a desolate dune in the deepest Sahara,
Like the Atlas Mountains in Algeria,
Like the Lakers winning the NBA Finals,
Like mom taking you to McDonald's, like a plan,

Like Japan, like Spam, like Amsterdam,
Like kissing the most beautiful girl, like gin,
Like riding a Huntington swell, like avoiding jail,
Like learning to spell, like the dandiest suit,
Like drinking champagne with Charlemagne,
Like L.A. without the smog, like beautiful ponds,
Like smooth operators on a phone sex line,
Like a five-year voyage to Mars, like a peacock,
Like still having a working cock, like clean socks,
Like dinosaurs when you're five years old,
Like Frank Sinatra has a cold, like *Esquire*,
Like an Armani suit and reading *GQ*,
Like *Sports Illustrated* circa 1982, like bees,
Like leaving the hospital after pulling through,
Like thinking about everything you like,
Like forgetting about clicks and dislikes,
Like reason without treason, like truth,
Like the Book of Ruth, like seasons,
Like snow in July on the Big Island, like teeth,
Like sermons and their blessings, like tears,
Like everything on this Earth, like worlds beyond,
Like sex for the first and every time,
Like the hunt for the sublime, like In-N-Out,
Like bikinis and apple pies, like surprises,
Like the principal's office, like blood, like sweat,
Like purple mountain majesties, like Union,
Like burning the Confederate flag, like noon,
Like a million times no, like a million yeses,
Like seeing your parents on the porch,
Like destiny, like urgency, like eternity,
Like...saying goodbye.

3:13 A.M.

Fast. Write the words. Hurry.
The clocks tick. The night sticks.
The halls of purity become stained.
Love is and will be made.

TEQUILA NEAT

I hope you wear that dress again.
You looked so beautiful.
Jose Cuervo and Tijuana, a pair.
We'll be more than drunken friends,
Frolic naked in the rain, sing songs,
Divulge secrets, laugh, kiss, fondle bliss,
Reticent things we haven't done dry.
You looked so beautiful.
We'll wake in a serene world,
Or never see another tomorrow.
Let's beam with bated breath,
Other nights, other bars, other drinks,
Lay the blueprint with a wink.
You looked so beautiful.
Another shot: Wouldn't that be neat?

THE LAST DAY OF MAY

Off yonder, past the windowpane,
Past visiting families, new babies,
Before the final feral orange streak
Blurs into pink, then purple,
A solitary cloud delineates
The boundary between the firmament,
The glint of God's eye, and the
Human realm, where darkness creeps.
The nurses and their charges,
The dutiful vigilantes in untold rooms,
Seek peace and possibility, hope,
Vaccines, the dominion of dreams.
Illuminated halls, doctors, buffed floors:
They are a union of joy, a party all their own.
I am among the well denizens, A Wing,
A tribe known to have the best of them.
Sometimes we cry, sometimes the crew.
Not oddly, the patients rarely do.
But today, the rules don't reign, we're
Slaves to the glow of TVs, phones,
The latest screens, the camaraderie.
Today, it's OK to breakdown, to weep.
It's the last day of May, and we can't sleep.

PINK

If pink is your favorite color,
Then I'm the Pink Panther.
I'm a blue suit and salmon tie.
I'm strawberry ice cream in July.
I am the pink of society,
The cotton-candy reign
Of aristocratic civilization.
I am deep kisses in Milan,
Pink sand beaches, and the
Santa Barbara mission.
I am coral, rose, blush, fuchsia,
Roseate, magenta, flesh.
I am pink films, Captain Pink,
I am pink nakedness,
Carved in debt to you.

PLEASURE

New definitions, missions, positions.

plea· sure | \ 'ple-zhər
1
: resurgent desire or inclination, that feeling of never going back, the first-time ejaculate, a trip to the Moon, water lilies in June
2
: the state where you find total elation, gratification, understand multiplication (conquering pain, stopping the rain, making it snow)
3
a
: sexual healing, erotic delectation, consented fantasies fulfilled (insert yours here)
b
: mindless distraction, diversion in illusion, denying sadness, or any other malady, an eternal embrace, completing a death-defying stunt

As in: He took pleasure in doing whatever he wanted before he died. (Pleasure, Kelvin C. Bias, 2025)

4
: a source of fun or contentment—that Norwegian girl, that Tijuana dress, that goal you scored, the words on the page

(The foliage of verbiage)

plea sured; plea sur ing *(transitive verb)*

1

: *to provide pleasure: SATISFY (especially a lover or significant other—insert names here:_____)*

2

: to provide sexual pleasure to *(perhaps yourself, perhaps that girl you once knew)*

insensitive/sensitive verb?

1

: *to take pleasure: a kick*

2

: *to wreak pleasure, to make it last, to step on the gas*

OTHER WORK BY KELVIN C. BIAS

MILKMAN (Novel)

What happens when everyman Calder Boyd starts to lactate? The Manhattanite becomes a media cause célèbre nicknamed the Milkman and old and new problems spill forth. The son of a former NBA star and a Norwegian artist, Calder copes with his strained marriage, losing his copywriting job at a boutique ad agency, a male-empowerment espousing mailman and a porn-star performance artist who wants to exploit him. He also deals with his late father's legacy and his wife's past indiscretion—all while breastfeeding their newborn daughter. Calder eventually becomes a pawn in the battle between a feminist organization and a militant men's society as he tries to become a better husband and man. The Fourth Estate, sex, art, love, memory, marriage and family converge during the snowiest winter on record in this commentary on contemporary American fatherhood.

WHISPERS OF A DYING SUN (Poetry)

These poems represent the vestiges of man from the perspective of a distant future. Akin to radio signals, the remnants of humanity streak toward a black hole where art, politics, love, technology, philosophy, science and the yearning for eternity accrete. Prophetic, stoic, polyphasic, the words disassemble and recombine on the other side in search of a new sun. I hope these poems find a closer home in your personal universe, heard but you're unsure of their origin, like whispers.

SEXOPOLIS: POEMS ON LOVE AND SEX

Love is a liberation, an act, a rebellion, a restriction, a communion. This poetry collection covers the universal topics of love and sex. From erotic to platonic and from marital to familial, love comes in many forms. We don't always get it, but we all crave it.

IMMACULATE DUST: LOVE POEMS

This poetry collection delves headlong into the world of love. Encompassing the realms of dream, fantasy and reality, the poems intend to engender not just love, but more pointedly, lovemaking. Lust. Love. Languor. These are three states of mind and body before, during and after the most pleasant poetry of human interaction: consented sex. We all possess desire, and we are all made of dust. Immaculate dust.

21 PARTICLES OF ETERNITY (Poetry)

Is eternity a quantifiable entity? An existence that can be divided into smaller particles, assembled and disassembled like a puzzle? Can it be bent? Borrowed? Recycled? Eternity is elusive. It constantly seems beyond our grasp yet always within our reach. *21 Particles of Eternity* covers topics as disparate as Mars and pornography and ranging from global warming and parenthood to politics and death.

The poet posits this: perhaps there are hidden portals where eternity can be glimpsed for fleeting moments, and the quest to find them brings meaning. How many particles will you find?

IF THE SKY IS AWAKE (Poetry)

Why do we have a 24-hour day, 60-minute hour, and 60-second minute? Thank the ancient Egyptians, Sumerians and Babylonians. Going further back, in humanity's early days, time was simply measured by the interval between sunrise and sunset. Today, we have much more precise methods. One second is defined as the duration of 9,192,631,770 periods of the radiation corresponding to the transition between the two hyperfine levels of the ground state of a cesium 133 atom. Confusing? Yes. Sometimes what transpires in daylight is the purest. Each day is a new dawn, a chance to reinvent yourself, find new love, rekindle an old one, and peer into the sky and feel awake. Reading poetry is like living life by your own clock. Lose yourself in your own sky.

THE LAST WILL & TESTAMENT OF THE UNITED STATES OF AMERICA: POETRY

This poetry collection conveys my anger and sadness over the current state of America—black, brown, yellow, red, white, and blue. On May 25, 2020—Memorial Day—a white woman named Amy Cooper walked her dog without a required leash in an area of Central Park known as the Ramble, and Christian Cooper, a peaceful, bird-watching black man, asked her to leash her dog. The legacy of slavery writ-large in the astounding fact they had the same surname. Amy responded by calling 911 to say that "an African American man" was threatening her and her dog. Christian calmly recorded the incident. (Imagine what might have happened if he hadn't.) The video went viral and provided a painful reminder of the tradition of white women falsely accusing black men of a crime. Later that night, in Minneapolis, Minnesota, a black man named George Floyd, who was not resisting arrest, was pressed face down into the pavement with a knee to his neck for nine minutes—*nine* minutes—by white Minneapolis police officer Derek Chauvin. Floyd died as he narrated his own death. "I can't breathe." Protests over Floyd's killing raged in cities across America for days, weeks...forever? On July 17, John Lewis, civil rights icon and Georgia Congressman, died from pancreatic cancer, and a few days before he passed, he wrote an essay to be released on the day of his funeral. On July 30, it ran in *The New York Times*. In his essay, Lewis wrote: "When you see something that is not right, you must say something. You must do something." *The Last Will & Testament of the United States of America* is the poet's way of saying and doing "something."

L.: POEMS

On May 13, 2020, I turned 50 years old. It was just another day. Just another day of worrying about my family, worrying about the state of the world, worrying about finding a job, worrying about COVID-19, and tantrums, and remote learning, wondering what I would do for the next 50 years, *if* I lived that long. To celebrate turning 50, to celebrate existence in general, I decided to write a poem for every year of my life. The process made me wonder: What have I truly accomplished in 50 years? Which begged another question. Is it important?

BLUE MILK: POEMS

Blue Milk is a mood: A concoction of poetry for your collection. The eighth book of poems by Kelvin C. Bias emerges from the idea of creating personal libations—with actual liquids or metaphorical ones. A drink may start with something as simple as a glass of milk, and end with something profound far beyond our blue planet. The choice is yours.

LIFEBLOOD (Poetry)

Love is the lifeblood of humanity. Enter this portal to desire, dreams, and destiny: a little red book.

THE LAST WILL & TESTAMENT OF THE UNITED STATES OF AMERICA: CODICIL EDITION

Poet Kelvin C. Bias adds 17 poems—indicting the Jan. 6 insurrection, mass shootings, and the rise of American fascism—in this Codicil version of the 2020 WILL of the United States of America.

IF YOU COULD BE EVERY COLOR (Poetry)

Aren't we more than just the visible spectrum of light? Our human eyes can detect wavelengths from 380 to 700 nanometers. What if we could see everything—below and beyond that range? What would we discover, about the universe and about ourselves? What will you uncover in *If You Could Be Every Color*?

NUDE BLUE (Poetry)

The word "blue" holds several meanings: the color, melancholy, learned, intellectual, Puritanical, profane, risqué, the sea, the sky, a Union soldier in the American Civil War, exasperated (blue in the face), unexpectedly (out of the blue), and even political affiliation. This naked collection of provocative poems encompasses blue in various shades.

DARLING: Poems

These poems embody thoughts whispered to your darling: confessions, dreams, desires, memories, fantasies—as if prying into a secret diary.

FEEDING GRAPES TO THE GODDESS: Poems

Feeding grapes to royalty is an ancient idea. Whether this is historically accurate is up for debate, nevertheless, anyone can partake. This collection of love poems hopes to stimulate such passionate action. Whom do you want to indulge?

WE DREAM HERE: Poems

Home is childhood, and childhood is home. Where you grew up, be it one place or many, and where you first dreamed, are places we often return to in adulthood. WE DREAM HERE is an aspiration and a philosophy.

ANGEL OF LOVE (Poetry)

Everyone needs a muse. Even muses. In this collection of love poems, everyone's a muse: jazz singers, suitors, old men, older women, antiquarians, insomniacs, masseuses, Vegas gamblers, and bygone Hollywood starlets. Who is your Angel of Love?

ABOUT THE AUTHOR

Kelvin C. Bias is a journalist, novelist, poet, filmmaker, and raconteur. However, his most important designation is father. He holds a B.A. in Political Science from the University of Arizona and an M.F.A in Screenwriting from NYU. He lives in New York City with his family.

www.ingramcontent.com/pod-product-compliance
Lightning Source LLC
Chambersburg PA
CBHW072147090426
42739CB00013B/3306